The Shakespeare Collection

HAMLET

RETOLD BY ANTHONY MASTERS

Illustrated by Stephen Player

HODDER
Wayland

an imprint of Hodder Children's Books

Character list:

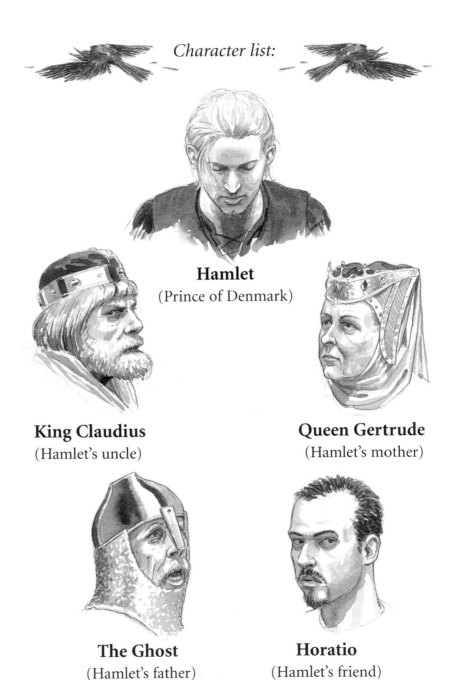

Hamlet
(Prince of Denmark)

King Claudius
(Hamlet's uncle)

Queen Gertrude
(Hamlet's mother)

The Ghost
(Hamlet's father)

Horatio
(Hamlet's friend)

Polonius
(Lord Chamberlain)

Ophelia
(Polonius's daughter)

Laertes
(Polonius's son)

Rosencrantz

Guildenstern

Marcellus

Barnardo

*T*he winter's night was bitterly cold and the sound of soldiers' boots rang out on the stone battlements of Elsinore Castle in Denmark.

Both of the soldiers on watch, Marcellus and Barnardo, were afraid. A ghost had been seen on the battlements and neither of them had believed their own eyes. But now Horatio, Prince Hamlet's closest friend, joined them.

"Horatio here says we imagined the ghost,"
explained Marcellus. "So I've asked him to share
our watch tonight. If the ghost appears again, he
can challenge it."

"It won't come." Horatio was convinced that
the soldiers were talking nonsense.

"Wait a minute," said Marcellus. "Surely
that's—" His voice faded away in terror as
a figure in armour began to walk across the
battlements.

"It's the ghost of the dead king," whispered
Barnardo.

*H*amlet, Crown Prince of Denmark, was in despair. His much-loved father had died from a poisonous snake bite. Then his mother, Queen Gertrude, had married his dead father's brother, Claudius, less than a month after the funeral! Hamlet was very suspicious.

"Why are you still so upset?" King Claudius asked him.

"Don't you think it's time you stopped wearing black?" Queen Gertrude pleaded. Hamlet was beginning to make her feel uneasy.

Hamlet couldn't bear to listen to either of them and turned away in disgust.

Alone and miserable, Hamlet muttered bitterly, "I wish I could kill myself. My father was such a wonderful man... And Claudius is the opposite! How could my mother have recovered from the king's death so quickly? My heart is breaking and I have to hold my tongue!"

Accompanied by Horatio, the two soldiers went nervously to Hamlet. They were both afraid that the moody prince would be angry with them, but knew that he should be told about the ghost.

Horatio did the talking. "Marcellus and Barnardo saw an armed figure walking on the battlements. They thought he looked like your father. Last night I joined them. I definitely saw the ghost of the dead king."

"Did you speak to it?" asked Hamlet, wide-eyed.

"Yes," said Horatio. "But dawn was breaking and a cock crowed. The ghost immediately vanished."

"I'll join you tonight. And if my father's ghost appears, I'll talk to him." Hamlet was deeply worried. *His father's ghost!* Something was terribly wrong if the old king's spirit was not at rest.

That night, Prince Hamlet joined Marcellus and Horatio on the battlements. They shivered as they gazed out across the raw winter landscape. The mist seemed to shift everywhere, gradually closing in.

Then a figure appeared beside them and Hamlet saw his father's dear face.

"Why have you left your grave?" whispered Hamlet.

The king beckoned to his son, seeming to want to talk to him alone. He led Hamlet further along the battlements.

"If you ever loved me," said the ghost, "you must avenge my murder."

Murder!

With a pounding heart, Hamlet listened as all his suspicions were confirmed.

"I was sleeping in the garden when Claudius crept up and poured poison into my ears. He murdered me and took my crown and then my wife."

Hamlet continued to listen with mounting anger as his father told of his agony about Claudius's betrayal. "But whatever you do to Claudius, you must never harm the queen," insisted the ghost. "Leave her to her own conscience."

Hamlet swore his revenge.

Then the air grew colder and the ghostly figure began to fade into the chilling mist.

Hamlet told Horatio and Marcellus not to mention the ghost to anyone. "And if I should behave strangely," he warned, "don't give me away."

*H*amlet did indeed begin to behave strangely.

"The Crown Prince came to see me," said Ophelia to her father, Polonius, the Lord Chamberlain of the court at Elsinore. "His eyes were wild and his clothes were torn and filthy. He stared at me and then went away again without speaking."

"Come and tell King Claudius," said Polonius. "I'm sure that Hamlet has gone mad with love for you. I should never have insisted that you refuse to see him."

But Hamlet was acting oddly with everyone. He talked in riddles and seemed to have completely lost his senses.

Claudius was bothered by Hamlet's sudden change of behaviour and he wanted to get to the bottom of it. He invited two childhood friends of Hamlet's, Rosencrantz and Guildenstern, to the court.

"We're worried that Hamlet is troubled by something much bigger than his father's death," Claudius told them. "See if you can persuade him to confide in you."

Rosencrantz and Guildenstern agreed that they would try. They were quite willing to betray Hamlet if it would please the king.

Just then Polonius bustled importantly into the room. He was certain that he knew what was wrong with Hamlet.

Claudius was not convinced, but Polonius had come up with a plan to see whether Hamlet's love for Ophelia had caused his madness.

"Ophelia can meet him by chance," Polonius told the king. "And you and I, my lord, can listen to their conversation from behind a curtain. Then we'll soon understand how Hamlet thinks."

When Rosencrantz and Guildenstern were brought to Hamlet, he was immediately suspicious of them.

"Why have you come to Elsinore?" he asked them.

"To visit you, of course," lied Rosencrantz.

"Tell me the truth," Hamlet insisted. "My uncle sent for you, didn't he?"

Uneasily, Guildenstern admitted that Hamlet was right. But he tried to distract the prince by telling him that a group of actors were coming to court.

Hamlet's face lit up, and a plan began to form in his mind...

"I'll get these players to act out the murder of my father," he said to himself when he was alone. "After all, the ghost could have been the devil himself trying to trick me into committing murder. If my uncle gets upset, then I'll know for certain that the ghost was speaking the truth."

Rosencrantz and Guildenstern reported back to the king and queen and Polonius that Hamlet had admitted he was feeling confused, but had refused to say why.

"However," said Rosencrantz. "He was very pleased to hear that the actors are coming to court. They're going to put on a play tonight."

"He'd like you and the queen to come, my lord," added Polonius. "But in the meantime, I'm going to ask Ophelia to encourage Hamlet to talk to her, so we can see what state of mind he's in."

The king and Polonius then hid so they could overhear the conversation.

$\mathcal{H}$amlet wandered through the passageway, deep in thought. It had been two months since he saw the ghost, and still he had not taken revenge. He was unaware that he was being watched and didn't at first notice that Ophelia was nearby.

"Whether or not to go on living, that's the question," Hamlet said to himself. "Why should I go through all this misery when I could just kill myself and end it all?" He paused. "But who knows what happens when we're dead? It might be even worse than this! The more I think about it, the harder it is to *do something...*"

Hamlet paced up and down, not knowing what to do. Then he saw Ophelia reading a prayer-book.

"Remember me in your prayers," Hamlet pleaded.

"How are you, my lord?" she asked gently.

Was Ophelia sent to trap him, too? Hamlet had always trusted her, but now he was not so sure. He began to act more strangely than before.

Then Ophelia tried to return all the letters and presents that Hamlet had given her and he got very angry indeed.

"You're just like my mother, always after men. Go and become a nun," he yelled at her savagely.

Ophelia was now certain that Hamlet was mad.

But the king was not convinced. When they came out of hiding he said to Polonius, "Hamlet certainly isn't mad with love for Ophelia. He's got something else on his mind. Something dangerous. I'm going to send him away to England on court business."

"I still think his problem is the result of Ophelia's rejection," insisted Polonius. "Why don't you ask his mother to talk to him privately after the play, and once again I'll hide and listen to what's said. If Queen Gertrude still can't find out what's the matter with him, then send him to England."

*U*naware of the trap that had been set for him,
Claudius sat down with the court to see the play.

Watching closely, Hamlet saw that both his
mother and uncle were looking uneasy as the play
continued, for the story was about the poisoning
of a king. Hamlet had written a new scene where
the murderer poured poison into the king's ears,
just as his father's ghost had told him. When this
happened, there was a great commotion.

"Stop the play!" shouted Polonius.

"Light, lights!" cried the king, storming out of the room.

Hamlet turned to Horatio. "Did you see how guilty my uncle looked at the very mention of poisoning?"

"I did indeed," replied Horatio.

*B*efore he could make up his mind what to do next, Hamlet was summoned to his mother's room.

"You've greatly offended your father," snapped Queen Gertrude.

"Mother – *you* have greatly offended *my* father, remarrying so soon – and to someone so unworthy," Hamlet quickly replied.

"You forget who you are talking to," said the queen angrily.

"No, I don't." Hamlet was bitter. "Just listen to what I have to say." He held his mother down in a chair and she cried out in fright.

"Help the queen!" shouted Polonius from his hiding place behind the curtains.

Hamlet thought that King Claudius himself was hiding there. Seizing his chance for revenge, he drew his sword and began to stab it through the curtains.

There was a cry and blood spurted.

When Hamlet dragged out the corpse, he discovered that he had killed Polonius.

Queen Gertrude was as horrified as her son. "You've committed murder," she cried.

"Even murder is not as bad as your behaviour," said Hamlet.

Suddenly the room became freezing cold. A chilly mist crept under the door and slowly filled the room. The mist began to form into the shape of a man, but only Hamlet could see his father's ghost.

"Are you angry that I haven't avenged you yet?" asked Hamlet.

"This visit *is* to spur you on," said the ghost. "But look, your mother is upset… You must speak to her, Hamlet."

Obediently, Hamlet turned to the queen and tried to reassure her, but she was terrified at the sight of him apparently talking to no one.

"Can't you see him?" Hamlet asked the queen. "It's my father. Look – he's leaving us."

But Queen Gertrude could see nothing and was sure that her son really was insane.

"Don't try to escape blame by saying I'm mad," shouted Hamlet. "Confess your sins and have nothing more to do with Claudius. Above all, don't tell him I'm sane or he'll be put on his guard against me."

"I can certainly promise you I won't do *that*," said the queen, as Hamlet left her.

After Polonius's murder, King Claudius had a good reason to send Hamlet to England with Rosencrantz and Guildenstern.

Once Hamlet had gone, Claudius muttered to himself, "And if you love me, King of England, you will carry out the wishes expressed in my letters – that Hamlet should be put to death."

But Hamlet had found the king's letters and managed to save himself. It was not long before Horatio received a note from his friend, explaining how he had made his escape:

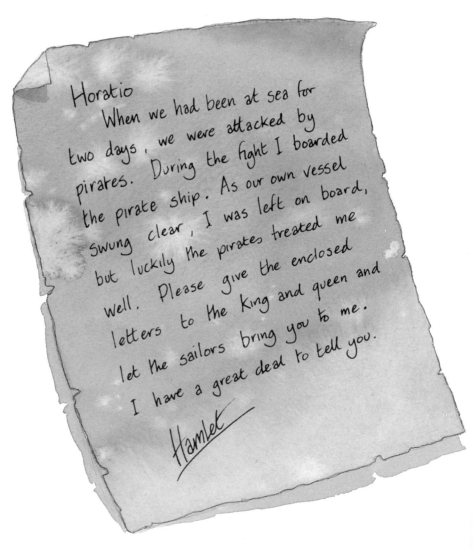

Horatio

When we had been at sea for two days, we were attacked by pirates. During the fight I boarded the pirate ship. As our own vessel swung clear, I was left on board, but luckily the pirates treated me well. Please give the enclosed letters to the King and queen and let the sailors bring you to me. I have a great deal to tell you.

Hamlet

When the king and queen received their letters, Claudius was afraid:

"High and mighty," his letter read. "I will see you tomorrow and explain in person why I have returned so unexpectedly and alone. Hamlet."

Claudius panicked and began to plot against Hamlet with Laertes, Polonius's son. Laertes was already in a white hot rage with Hamlet for killing his father, and for driving his sister out of her mind. When she was told that Hamlet had murdered her father, Ophelia went mad with grief – and her madness was real.

"Hamlet's returning," Claudius told him. "Do you really want to avenge your father's death?"

"I'll kill him *anywhere*," Laertes promised him.

Claudius was pleased at Laertes's fury. Surely here was the man who could kill the prince. "When Hamlet gets back, I'll praise your skill as a swordsman. He's bound to challenge you to a duel. If you use a sharpened sword, I'm sure you can easily kill him."

"Of course I'll kill him," said Laertes eagerly. "I'll poison the tip of my sword, too. He'll die from the slightest scratch."

"I'll also have a poisoned drink ready for him," Claudius assured Laertes. "If he escapes your sword and calls for a drink, then I can kill him."

Their plotting was interrupted by Queen Gertrude who brought terrible news. In her madness, Ophelia had fallen into the river and drowned.

Claudius realized this tragedy would greatly work in his favour, particularly when he saw Laertes's grief. "I was trying to calm Laertes down," Claudius said cunningly to the queen. "Now I fear his rage will break out again."

When Hamlet arrived back at Elsinore, he saw that a new grave had been dug in the churchyard. He watched as the mourners drew near, bearing Ophelia's body. Pain flooded through him.

Laertes was in a terrible state, and during the funeral he leapt into the grave, pleading with the attendants to bury him along with his sister.

Hamlet was furious that Laertes should show such love and grief for Ophelia. What about his own love? His own grief? Angry and upset, he pushed through the mourners and leapt into the grave himself.

"The devil take your soul," cried Laertes and the two young men began to fight.

"Drag them apart," snarled Claudius, and his men ran to separate Hamlet and Laertes.

"I loved Ophelia," Hamlet cried. "Forty thousand brothers couldn't love her as I did."

"Remember our plans," Claudius quietly reminded Laertes.

The sword fight between Hamlet and Laertes began in front of the entire court.

The king had put out two glasses of wine and said he would be drinking to Hamlet's victory.

Hamlet had a couple of hits and Claudius drank a toast to his skills as a swordsman. So did Queen Gertrude – but she drank from the poisoned glass.

Suddenly, Laertes hit Hamlet with the sharp
point of his poisoned sword. It drew blood.

Angry that the sword had been sharpened,
Hamlet sprang at Laertes, making him drop his
sword. In the scuffle, Hamlet picked up the
poisoned blade and thrust it through Laertes.

Then Hamlet saw that the queen was slipping from her throne.

"What's the matter with her?" Hamlet gasped.

"She's fainted at the sight of so much blood," said Claudius hurriedly.

But the queen was still conscious. "It was the wine," she groaned. "I've been poisoned."

Hamlet turned to the guards. "Shut the castle gates," he commanded. "No one is to leave."

"Wait," muttered Laertes. "I've got a confession to make – I poisoned the tip of my sword. You haven't got long to live – and neither have I." Already Laertes was beginning to feel the effects of the poison. He fell to the ground, shouting, "It's the king's fault!"

Realizing that he had little time left, Hamlet
flew at his uncle and thrust the sword into his
heart. Then he forced the rest of the poisoned
wine down the king's throat.

At long last Hamlet had fulfilled the promise
he had made to his father's ghost.

As Hamlet also fell to the ground, Horatio
rushed over and knelt down beside him.

"Horatio, my dear friend. You are the only one left," whispered Hamlet. "You have to tell the world the story of this tragedy." And with that, Hamlet was dead.

Broken-hearted, Horatio stood surrounded by the bodies of Gertrude, Laertes, Claudius and Hamlet. The tragedy was complete.

The Shakespeare Collection

Look out for these other titles in the Shakespeare Collection:

The Tempest Retold by Chris Powling
After a terrible storm, a ship lies wrecked on Prospero's island.
But the storm was no coincidence... Propsero the magician has
revenge on his mind, and when there's magic in the air,
anything can happen!

Twelfth Night Retold by Jan Dean
Love is in the air... The duke is in love with Olivia, who's in
love with his manservant, Cesario. The trouble is, Cesario is
really a woman in disguise – and she's in love with the duke!
Will the course of true love ever run smooth?

Antony and Cleopatra Retold by Kathy Elgin
Antony was once the bravest general of the Roman Empire...
That is, until he fell in love with Cleopatra. With war in the air
and the Empire falling apart, can Antony put everything right,
or will it all end in disaster?

You can buy all these books from your local bookseller, or
order them direct from the publisher. For more information
about The Shakespeare Collection, write to: *The Sales
Department, Hodder Children's Books, a division of Hodder
Headline Limited, 338 Euston Road, London NW1 3BH.*